A NOTE TO PARENTS

When your children are ready to "step into reading," giving them the right books is as crucial as giving them the right food to eat. **Step into Reading Books** present exciting stories and information reinforced with lively, colorful illustrations that make learning to read fun, satisfying, and worthwhile. They are priced so that acquiring an entire library of them is affordable. And they are beginning readers with a difference—they're written on five levels.

Early Step into Reading Books are designed for brand-new readers, with large type and only one or two lines of very simple text per page. **Step 1 Books** feature the same easy-to-read type as the Early Step into Reading Books, but with more words per page. **Step 2 Books** are both longer and slightly more difficult, while **Step 3 Books** introduce readers to paragraphs and fully developed plot lines. **Step 4 Books** offer exciting nonfiction for the increasingly independent reader.

The grade levels assigned to the five steps—preschool through kindergarten for the Early Books, preschool through grade 1 for Step 1, grades 1 through 3 for Step 2, grades 2 through 3 for Step 3, and grades 2 through 4 for Step 4—are intended only as guides. Some children move through all five steps very rapidly; others climb the steps over a period of several years. Either way, these books will help your child "step into reading" in style!

Library of Congress Cataloging-in-Publication Data
Milton, Joyce. Bears are curious / by Joyce Milton ; illustrated by Christopher Santoro.
p. cm. — (Step into reading. Step 1 book)
SUMMARY: Discusses different types of bears, focusing especially on the period when the mother
comes out of hibernation with new cubs, describing how they hunt for food, what they eat, and how
the mother protects her young.
ISBN 0-679-85301-4 (pbk.) — ISBN 0-679-95301-9 (lib. bdg.) 1. Bears—Behavior—Juvenile literature.
[1. Bears.] I. Santoro, Christopher, ill. II. Title. III. Series: Step into reading. Step 1 book. QL737.C27M57
1998 [E]—dc21 97-26757

www.randomhouse.com/kids

Printed in the United States of America 10 9 8 7 6 5
STEP INTO READING is a registered trademark of Random House, Inc.

Step into Reading®

BEARS ARE CURIOUS

By Joyce Milton
Illustrated by Christopher Santoro

A Step 1 Book

Random House 🏠 New York

Bears are curious.
They are almost always
hungry, too.

This mother bear
and her cubs
are looking for
something good to eat.

The mother bear
sniffs the air.
Her nose tells her
that bees are living
in the hollow tree.

She sticks her paw
inside the tree
and scoops up
some sweet wild honey.

A few bees are stuck
in the honey.
The mother bear
gobbles them up!

The cubs lick honey
from their mother's paw.
Angry bees buzz around.
But the bears' thick fur
keeps them safe.

Why are the bears
so hungry?

All winter long,
the mother bear
stayed in a small cave.
She didn't eat
anything at all.

One winter day,
her cubs were born.
The cubs drank
their mother's milk.

Mother and cubs
snuggled together
to keep warm.
Most of the time,
they slept.

Then spring came.
The mother bear was
thin and hungry.

She needed to find food
for herself and her cubs.

A hungry bear will eat almost anything . . .

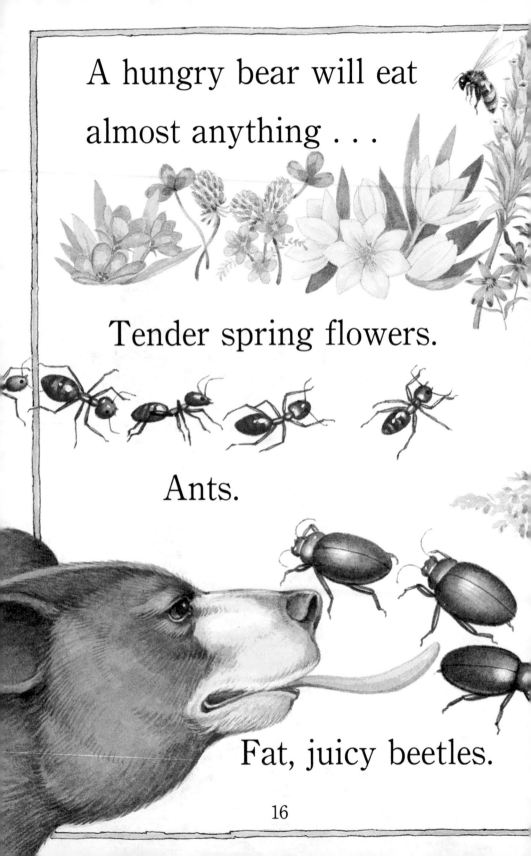

Tender spring flowers.

Ants.

Fat, juicy beetles.

Acorns.

Berries.

Sometimes they even

catch mice.

All summer long,
the cubs follow
their mother.
She protects them
from danger.

One day, an eagle
swoops down
at one of the cubs.
The mother bear
comes running.

She is just in time!

By autumn,
the mother bear
is fat again.
The cubs are fat, too.
They will spend
one more winter together.

There are different
kinds of bears.
The mother and her cubs
are black bears.
Black bears are good
at climbing trees.

Brown bears are bigger
than black bears.
They have longer claws.

Sometimes they are called
grizzly bears.

Some bears catch fish.

This cub is still learning.

He does a belly flop
right on top of a fish.

Oops!

The fish got away.

Polar bears live
in the Arctic,
a land of ice and snow.
Their thick fur
keeps them warm.

Polar bears are
great swimmers.
They hunt seals
and walruses.

Young bears like to roam.
Sometimes they wander
into towns.
Then their curiosity
can get them into trouble.

One showed up at a
backyard birthday party.
The cake was tasty!
But where were the guests?
They had all run away!

But bears *are* wild.

When they mix with people,

they can be dangerous.

This bear was lucky.

A ranger shot it

with a special dart.

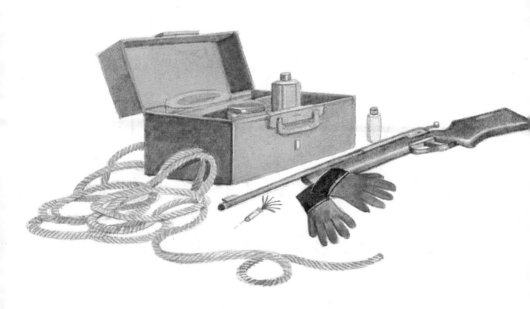

The bear wasn't hurt.
He just fell asleep.
Rangers loaded him
into a truck.

When the bear woke up,
he was back in the woods.
Right where he belonged.